Sing A Song Of Africa

Caroline Hooper

Illustrated by David Meldrum

Chester Music Limited
Part of The Music Sales Group
14-15 Berners Street, London W1T 3LJ

Contents

Cover design by Chloë Alexander
Printed by MPG Printwise Limited

Order No. CH61675   ISBN 978-0-7119-8313-7

Tangishaka

1. Tan - gi - sha - ka yan - tu - mye Ho - ra! se _____ wan - du - hu - ye.

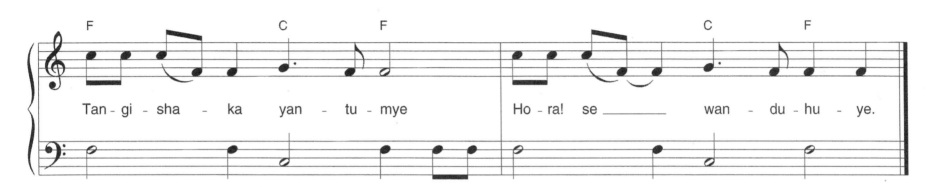

Tan - gi - sha - ka yan - tu - mye Ho - ra! se _____ wan - du - hu - ye.

Tangishaka is a God.

1. Tangishaka yantumye
   Hora! se wanduhuye.

2. Shikura inkoni,
   Twingine ibibondo.

3. Izo ni inyambo,
   Ntizimirwa.

4. Iyi ningeri za Buyenzi
   Sukiranyi z'amazi.

In this song a woman thanks Tangishaka for giving her a child.

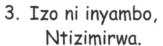

Nobody Knows The Trouble I See

This is a type of song called a Spiritual.

Spirituals were originally sung by slaves taken from Africa to America.

Nobody knows the trouble I see,
Nobody knows my sorrow;
Nobody knows the trouble I see,
Glory halleluia!

1. Sometimes I'm up, sometimes I'm down,
Oh, yes, Lord!
Sometimes I'm almost to the groun',
Oh, yes, Lord!

Nobody knows the trouble I see...

2. Altho' you see me going 'long,
Oh, yes, Lord!
I have my troubles here below,
Oh, yes, Lord!

Nobody knows the trouble I see...

3. What makes old Satan hate me so,
Oh, yes, Lord!
Cause he got me once and let me go,
Oh, yes, Lord!

Nobody knows the trouble I see...

Ssemusota

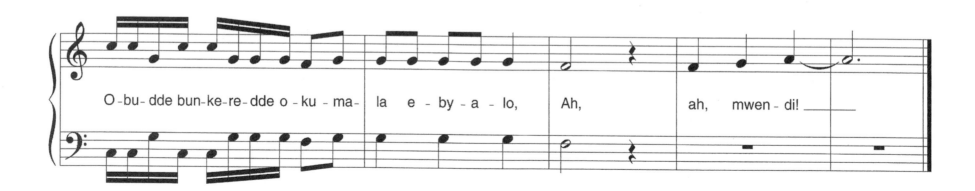

I'm Goin' Chop Crab

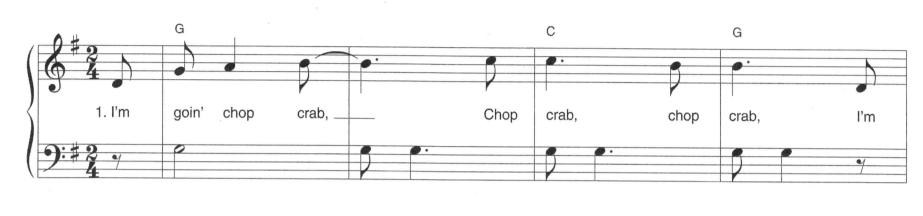

1. I'm goin' chop crab, Chop crab, chop crab, I'm

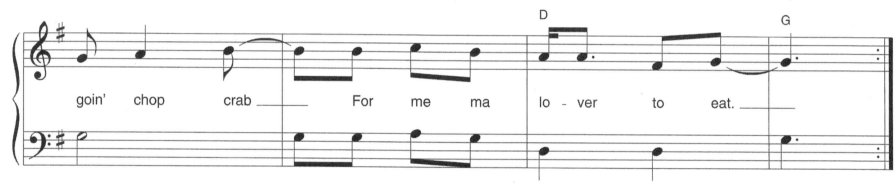

goin' chop crab For me ma lo – ver to eat.

1. I'm goin' chop crab,
   Crab, crab,
   I'm goin' chop crab
   For me ma lover to eat.

2. I'm goin' dig gold,
   Dig gold, dig gold,
   I'm goin' dig gold
   For me ma lover to live.

3. I'm goin' plant farm,
   Plant farm, plant farm,
   I'm goin' plant farm
   For me ma lover to eat.

4. I'm goin' dig stone,
   Dig stone, dig stone,
   I'm goin' dig stone
   For me ma lover to sell.

5. I'm goin' build house,
   Build house, build house,
   I'm goin' build house
   For me ma lover to sleep.

6. I'm goin' buy car,
   Buy car, buy car,
   I'm goin' buy car
   For me ma lover to ride.

Tole Ya Wati

1. To - le, to - le, to - le, to - le ya wa - ti, Ki -

- ya bi - la - tin ma - li, _____ Ki - ya bi - la - tin ma - li. *Ya da -*

This tune is in 2/4 time and 3/4 time, so count very carefully!

1. Tole, tole, tole, tole ya wati,
   Kiya bilatin mali,
   Kiya bilatin mali.

   Ya dabale,
   Ya dabale, balule,
   Ya dabale, balule,
   Ya dabale, balule.

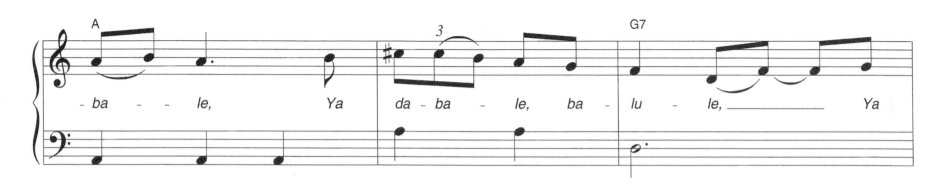

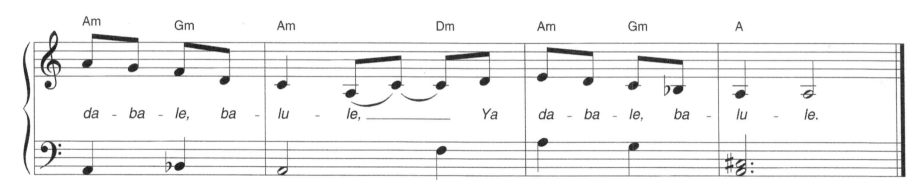

2. Ya mucayo ati hin duftu,
   Ani kaze galure,
   Ani kaze galure.

   Ya dabale...

In Ethiopia, Tole ya means "thank you".

Aunt Hessie's White Horse

Traditional

Can't you see Aunt Hessie's white horse,
Aunt Hessie's white horse,
Aunt Hessie's white horse,
Oh can't you see Aunt Hessie's white horse,
And gee-up a trot for me?

Don't you call him slow,
Aunt Hessie will make him go;
He'll gallop along so fine,
He'll make the whole world mine.

Oh, can't you see Aunt Hessie's white horse...

Khoë Li

Khoë li ke ela
Toloka, toloka.
Ha ena mosa
Toloka, toloka.
Mosa oa eona
Toloka, toloka.
Eka oa n tja
Toloka, toloka.

Khoë li means "the moon".

Lines 1, 3, 5 and 7 are usually sung by one person. The others are sung by a group of people.

Kumbaya

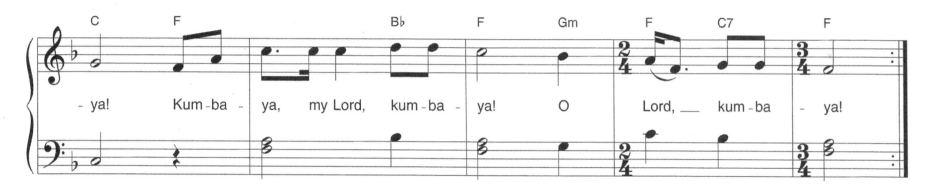

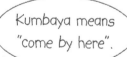

Kumbaya means "come by here".

1. Kumbaya, my Lord, kumbaya!
   Kumbaya, my Lord, kumbaya!
   Kumbaya, my Lord, kumbaya!
   O Lord, kumbaya!

2. Someone's crying Lord, kumbaya!
   Someone's crying Lord, kumbaya!
   Someone's crying Lord, kumbaya!
   O Lord, kumbaya!

3. Someone's singing Lord, kumbaya!
   Someone's singing Lord, kumbaya!
   Someone's singing Lord, kumbaya!
   O Lord, kumbaya!

4. Someone's praying Lord, kumbaya!
   Someone's praying Lord, kumbaya!
   Someone's praying Lord, kumbaya!
   O Lord, kumbaya!

Steal Away

Steal a - way, steal a - way, Steal a - way to Je - sus! Steal a - way, steal a - way home, I

ain't got long to stay here. 1. My Lord _____ calls me, He calls me by the

thun - der; The trum - pet sounds with - in - a my soul: I ain't got long to stay here.

Steal away, steal away,
Steal away to Jesus!
Steal away, steal away home,
I ain't got long to stay here.

Steal away means to go very quietly.

1. My Lord calls me,
He calls me by the thunder;
The trumpet sounds within-a my soul:
I ain't got long to stay here.

2. Green trees are bending,
Poor sinners stand a trembling;
The trumpet sounds within-a my soul:
I ain't got long to stay here.

3. My Lord calls me,
He calls me by the lightning;
The trumpet sounds within-a my soul:
I ain't got long to stay here.

Mfene Sandhleni

Deep River

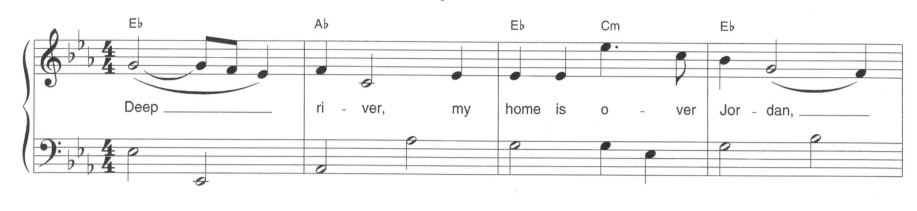

Deep _____ ri - ver, my home is o - ver Jor - dan, _____

Deep _____ ri - ver, Lord, I want to cross o - ver in - to camp - ground.

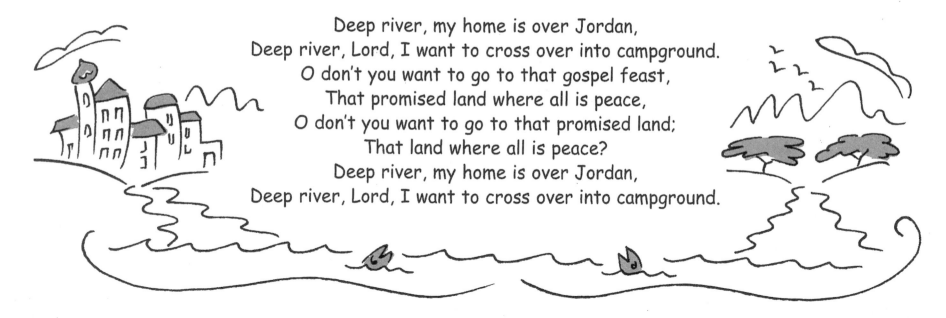

Deep river, my home is over Jordan,
Deep river, Lord, I want to cross over into campground.
O don't you want to go to that gospel feast,
That promised land where all is peace,
O don't you want to go to that promised land;
That land where all is peace?
Deep river, my home is over Jordan,
Deep river, Lord, I want to cross over into campground.

Rana Djinak

Rana djinak Yadou aïni;
Rana djinak, Nari! Yanari!
Rana djinak Yadou aïni;
Rana djinak, Nari! Yanari!

This is a blessing, a type of prayer.

Little David

Little David, play on your harp,
Hallelu! Hallelu!
Little David, play on your harp,
Hallelu!

1. Little David was a shepherd boy,
He killed Goliath, and shouted for joy.

Little David, play on your harp...

2. Done told you once, done told you twice,
There're sinners in hell for shooting dice.

Little David, play on your harp...

3. Joshua was the son of Nun,
He never would quit till the work was done.

Little David, play on your harp...

Ozibane! Ozibane! Ozibane!

A wiggly line between two notes tells you to slide gradually from one note to the next.

As you slide between the two notes in the last line, you sing "wîi", pronouced "weeeee".

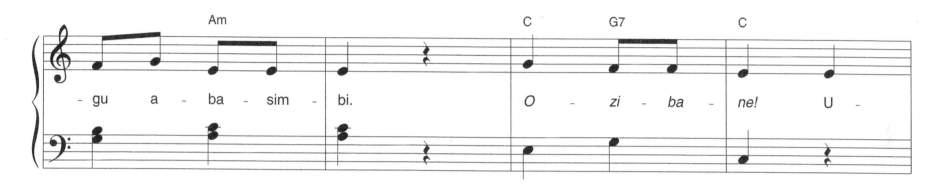

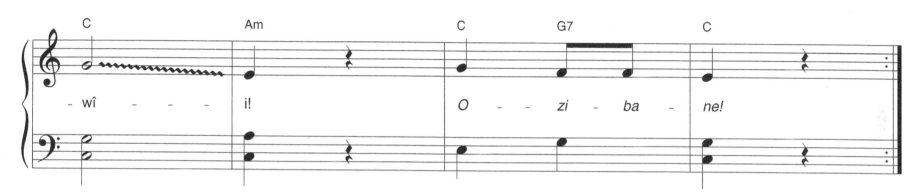

Ozibane, zibane, zibane!
Ozibane!
Kanga sulwe bâmutunga ubulungu kumulonga.
Ozibane!
Kanga sulwe bâmutunga ubulungu abasimbi.
Ozibane!
Uwîi!
Ozibane!

One person sings the 1st, 3rd, 5th and 7th lines. Everyone else joins in to sing "Ozibane!".

Down By The Riverside

You could have one person singing the 1st and 5th lines of each verse, with everyone else joining in for the rest.

1. I'm gonna lay down my burden,
   Down by the riverside,
   Down by the riverside,
   Down by the riverside.
   I'm gonna lay down my burden,
   Down by the riverside,
   Ain't gonna study war no more.

   Ain't gonna study war no more,
   Ain't gonna study war no more,
   No I ain't gonna study war no more.

2. I'm gonna lay down my sword an' shield,
       Down by the riverside,
       Down by the riverside,
       Down by the riverside.
    I'm gonna lay down my sword an' shield,
       Down by the riverside,
    Ain't gonna study war no more.

    Ain't gonna study war no more...

3. I'm gonna try on my long white robe,
       Down by the riverside,
       Down by the riverside,
       Down by the riverside.
    I'm gonna try on my long white robe,
       Down by the riverside,
    Ain't gonna study war no more.

    Ain't gonna study war no more...

Fhola Li Na Mulanda

Fho-la li na mu-lan-du! Yo-vhe, li na mu-lan-du! Nde-ndi to-ta fho-la Yo-vhe, li na mu-lan-du!

Tshan-da tsha Ga-ba-ra, Yo-vhe, li na mu-lan-du! La rhu-ya la sen-ga. Yo-vhe, li na mu-lan-du!

Fhola li na mulandu!
Yovhe, li na mulandu!
Ndendi tota fhola
Yovhe, li na mulandu!
Tshanda tsha Gabara,
Yovhe, li na mulandu!
La rhuya la senga.
Yovhe, li na mulandu!

Joshua Fit The Battle Of Jericho

Joshua fit the battle of Jericho,
Jericho, Jericho,
Joshua fit the battle of Jericho,
And the walls came tumblin' down.

You may talk about your King of Gideon,
You may talk about your man of Saul,
But there's none like good old Joshua,
At the battle of Jericho.

Joshua fit the battle of Jericho...

Gbodi

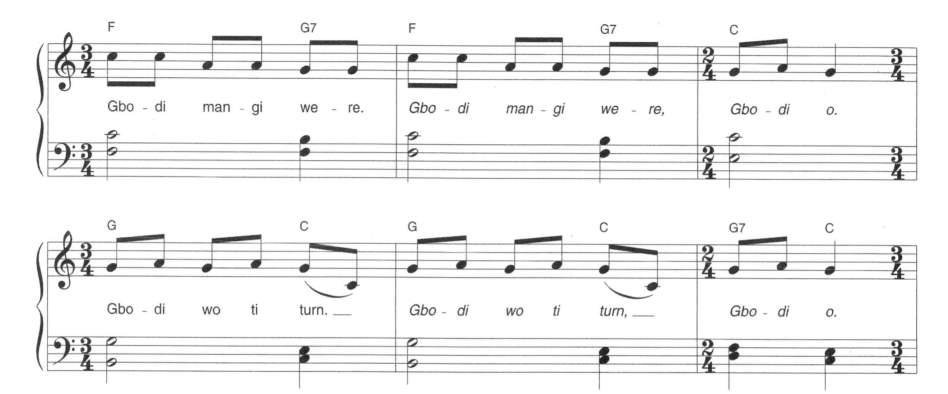

Gbo - di   man - gi   we - re.

Gbo - di   man - gi   we - re,

Gbo - di   o.

Gbo - di   wo   ti   turn. __

Gbo - di   wo   ti   turn, __

Gbo - di   o.

Gbodi mangi were.
Gbodi mangi were, Gbodi o.
Gbodi wo ti turn.
Gbodi wo ti turn, Gbodi o.
Gbodi gu a gu.
Gbodi gu a gu, Gbodi o.
Gbodi sungun sende.
Gbodi sungun sende, Gbodi o.
Gbodi guari.
Gbodi guari, Gbodi o.

Hush! Somebody's Calling My Name

Sing the chorus as quietly as you can.

Hush! Hush! Somebody's calling my name;
Hush! Hush! Somebody's calling my name;
Hush! Hush! Somebody's calling my name;
O my Lord, O my Lord, what shall I do?

1. I'm so glad that trouble don't last always;
   I'm so glad that trouble don't last always;
   I'm so glad that trouble don't last always;
   I'm so glad that trouble don't last always;
   O my Lord, O my Lord, what shall I do?

   Hush! Hush! Somebody's calling my name...

2. I'm so glad I got my religion in time;
   I'm so glad I got my religion in time;
   I'm so glad I got my religion in time;
   O my Lord, O my Lord, what shall I do?

   Hush! Hush! Somebody's calling my name...

3. I'm so glad my soul's got a hiding place;
   I'm so glad my soul's got a hiding place;
   I'm so glad my soul's got a hiding place;
   I'm so glad my soul's got a hiding place;
   O my Lord, O my Lord, what shall I do?

   Hush! Hush! Somebody's calling my name...

Imandwa

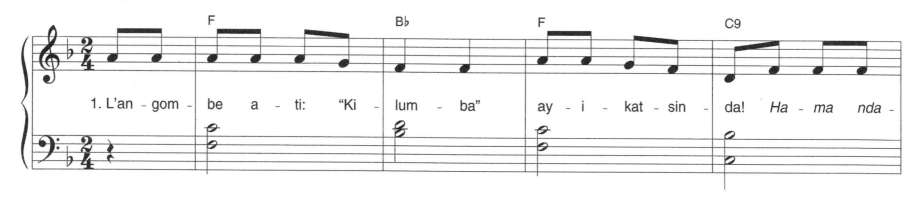

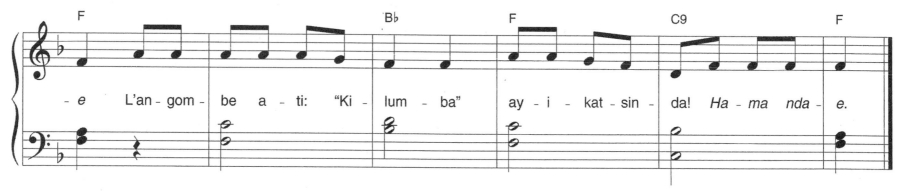

The first line of each verse should be sung by one person.

The second line is like a chorus.

1. L'angombe ati: "Kilumba", ayikatsinda!
    Hama ndaže.

2. Ati ikxanze ndaswandalika, ayikatsinda!
    Hama ndaže.

3. Binego ati: "Kilumba", ayikatsinda!
    Hama ndaže.

4. Ati ikxanze ndaswandalika, ayikatsinda!
    Hama ndaže.

Ny O L'on Nanacy

Ny-o lon' na-na-ry, N'za-za kam-bo-ty, At-ao-ny toa tsy-a-dry, F'za-za kam-bo-ty.

Mba as-kaiz' ian-tra-na re-o. Rah! ma-ty I-kam-bo-ty. Ha ha sam-ba-tra-na re-o. Ny han-de-vin a-zy.

Nyo lon' nanary,
N'zaza kamboty,
Ataony toa tsyadry,
F'zaza kamboty.
Mba askaiz' iantrana reo.
Rah! Maty Ikamboty.
Ha ha sambatrana reo.
Ny handevin azy.

This is another 'call-and-response' song.

É, Ie, Ie

É, ie, ie, mo-tu-le-ne Li no lion ku la ma mua ku mon - go.

Ka la ka la na zin dum - ba na ba tuem - be. A a!

Non go - ro oa sham ba zan gom - be. A a!

É, ie, ie, motulene
Li no lion kula ma mua ku mongo.
Ka la ka la na zin dumba na ba tuembe.
A a!
Non goro oa sham ba zan gombe.
A a!

Go Down, Moses

1. When Is - rael was in E - gypt's land; Let my peo - ple go, Op - pressed so hard they

could not stand; Let my peo - ple go. Go down, Mo - ses, Way down in

E - gypt's land, __ Tell __ ole Pha - raoh, Let my peo - ple go.

You can sing this as a 'call-and-response' song if you like.

Everyone joins in to sing "Let my people go".

1.   When Israel was in Egypt's land;
Let my people go,
Oppressed so hard they could not stand;
Let my people go.

*Go down, Moses,
Way down in Egypt's land,
Tell ole Pharaoh,
Let my people go.*

2.   Thus saith the Lord, bold Moses said,
Let my people go,
If not, I'll smite your first-born dead,
Let my people go.

Go down, Moses...

3.   No more shall they in bondage toil,
Let my people go,
If them come out with Egypt spoil,
Let my people go.

Go down, Moses...

4.   O let us all from bondage flee,
Let my people go,
And let us all in Christ be free,
Let my people go.

Go down, Moses...

Manthi'ki

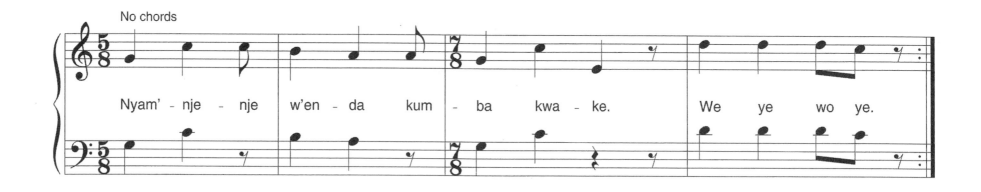

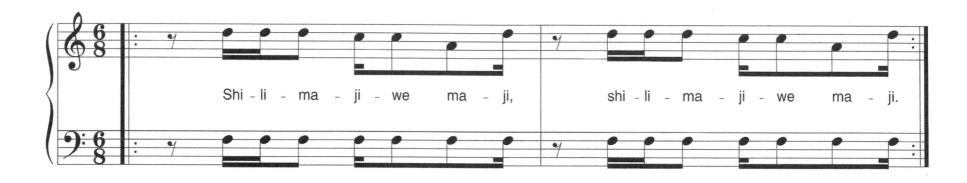

Nyam'njenje w'enda kumba kwake.
We ye wo ye.
Nyam'njenje w'enda kumba kwake.
We ye wo ye.
Shilimajiwe maji, shilimajiwe maji,
Shilimajiwe maji, shilimajiwe maji.
Shili mb'luka, mb'luka, shili,
Mb'luka, mb'luka, shili,
Mb'luka, mb'luka.
Wensia! Wensia!

Mofe Moni S'mo Ho Gbeke

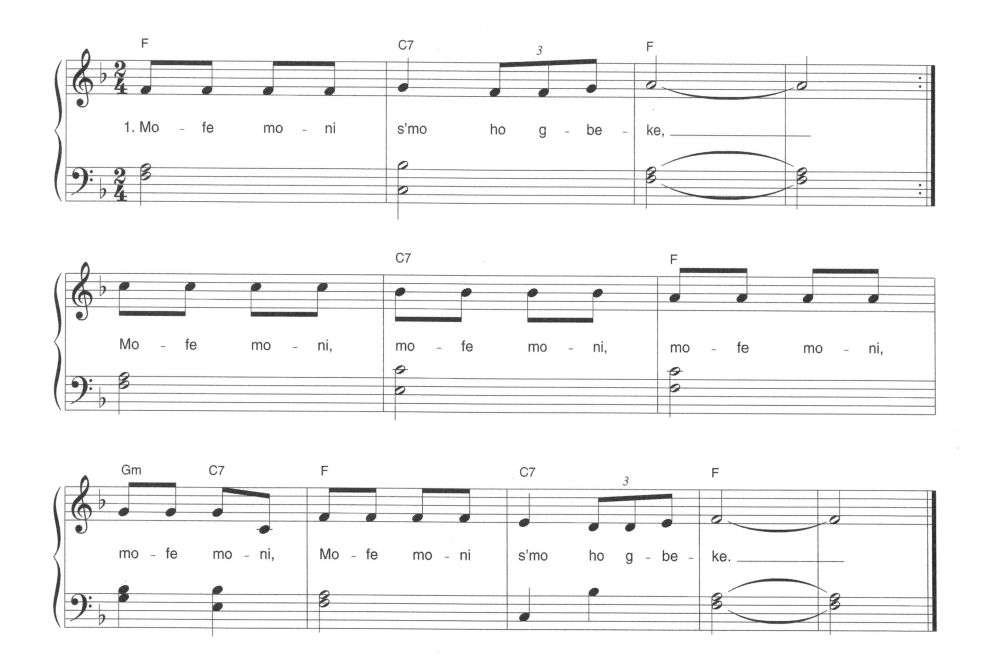

1. Mofe moni s'mo ho gbeke,
Mofe moni, mofe moni, mofe moni, mofe moni,
Mofe moni s'mo ho gbeke.

In this song, each verse uses the same words, sung in a different language.

2. Ev'rybody loves Saturday night,
Ev'rybody, ev'rybody, ev'rybody, ev'rybody,
Everybody loves Saturday night.

In French...

3. Tout le monde aime samedi soir,
Tout le monde, tout le monde, tout le monde, tout le monde,
Tout le monde aime samedi soir.

In Italian...

4. Piace a tutti sabato sera,
Piace a tutti, piace a tutti, piace a tutti, piace a tutti,
Piace a tutti sabato sera.

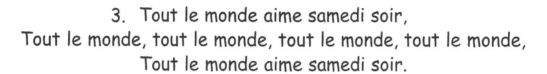

5. Nos gústa a tódos la nóche de sábado,
Nos gústa a tódos, nos gústa a tódos, nos gústa a tódos, nos gústa a tódos,
Nos gústa a tódos la nóche de sábado.

In Spanish...

6. Jeder freut sich auf Samstag Abend,
Jeder freut sich, jeder freut sich, jeder freut sich, jeder freut sich,
Jeder freut sich auf Samstag Abend.

In German...

Shellilà Shek

Shellilà shek means "our great leader"

Shellilà shek Mohammed Sahleh
Almadadio, Mohammed Sahleh.
Shellilà shek Mohammed Sahleh
Almadadio, Mohammed Sahleh.

8/11 (179109)